Puppy's First Year Keepsake Book

Capture the special moments!

*Until one has loved a puppy or dog a part
of one's heart remains unawakened.*

A baby book to document
your dog's life as it happens!

*Puppies and dogs are earthly miracles with wagging tails,
little hearts full of love and the pitter-patter of paws.*

Puppy's First Year

A baby book for your puppy or dog to keep heart filled memories and photos of special moments with your dog. There is space for snapshots of your puppy! This blank baby book gives dog lovers a place to chart their puppy's growth.

As your puppy grows into an adult you can create a book full of memories and capture the special moments.

There is a page for your puppy's first birthday, first Christmas, first bath plus birth information. Keep track of your puppy's vaccine records and health.

There is even a page to place your puppy's paw prints!

You can take photos of your dog discovering his world as he grows into an adult.

Pictures are worth a thousand words, it helps us remember the little moments that bring us such joy in an instant.

Don't miss the special times when your puppy or dog is sleeping, bounding across the yard, his first birthday or favorite things to do! With this dog baby book you will be able to keep your favorite memories to enjoy the happy moments for years!

Start creating lasting memories today of your puppy or dog!

Yesterday I was a puppy.

Today I'm a puppy.

Tomorrow I'll probably still be a puppy.

Sigh! There's so little hope for advancement.

My First Day Home

Date I joined my new family: _April 2, 2015_

First Photo

My First Week Home

My Birthday: _____

Place of Birth: _____

Fur and Markings: _____

My Name: _____

I'm growing. How much did I grow!

Age	Lbs	Oz
6 Weeks		
8 Weeks		
10 Weeks		
3 Months		
4 Months		
6 Months		
8 Months		
10 Months		
1 Year		
2 Years		

Puppy Paw Print

Adult Paw Print

My Favorite Person

Photo Here

_____

_____

_____

_____

_____

My First Bath

Photo Here

_____

_____

_____

_____

_____

My Favorite Food

Photo Here

_____

_____

_____

_____

My Favorite Toy

Photo Here

_____

_____

_____

_____

_____

My First Birthday

Photo Here

_____

_____

_____

_____

_____

My First Christmas

Photo Here

_____

_____

_____

_____

_____

Vaccination Records

Age	Date	Distemper	Parvo	Rabies	Deworm
6 weeks					
10 weeks					
14 weeks					
1 Year					
2 Years					
3 Years					
4 Years					
5 Years					
6 Years					
7 Years					
8 Years					
9 Years					
10 Years					
11 Years					
12 Years					

Heartworm Testing:

1 Year___   2 Year___   3 Year ___   4 Year___ 5 Year___

6 Year___   7 Year___   8 Year ___   9 Year___ 10 Year___

Medical Record Notes:

Medical Record Notes:

_____

_____

_____

_____

_____

_____

_____

_____

Medical Record Notes:

_____

_____

_____

_____

_____

_____

_____

_____

_____

Medical Record Notes:

_____

_____

_____

_____

_____

_____

_____

_____

_____

_____

Medical Treatments:

Neutered	Spayed	Other

Medical Conditions:

Date	Accidents or Injuries

Medical Emergencies:

_____

_____

_____

_____

_____

_____

_____

_____

_____

Medical Emergencies:

_____

_____

_____

_____

_____

_____

_____

_____

_____

The Puppy Days

Don't miss the happy moments!
Start creating lasting memories today!

Our Puppy

Photo Here

Our Puppy

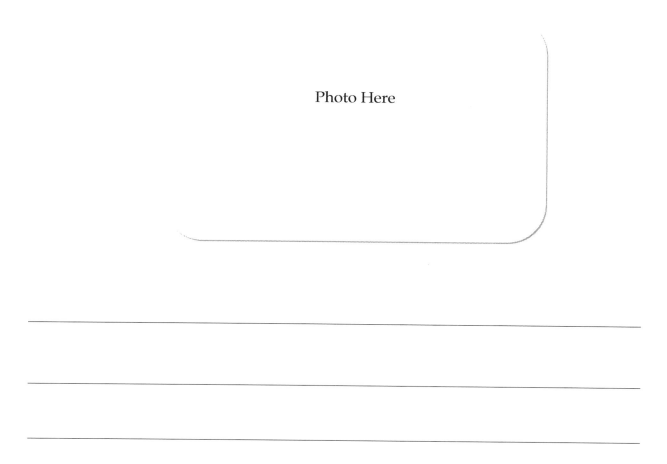

Photo Here

Our Puppy

Photo Here

Our Puppy

Photo Here

_____

_____

_____

Our Puppy

Photo Here

Our Puppy

Photo Here

Our Puppy

Photo Here

_____

_____

_____

Our Puppy

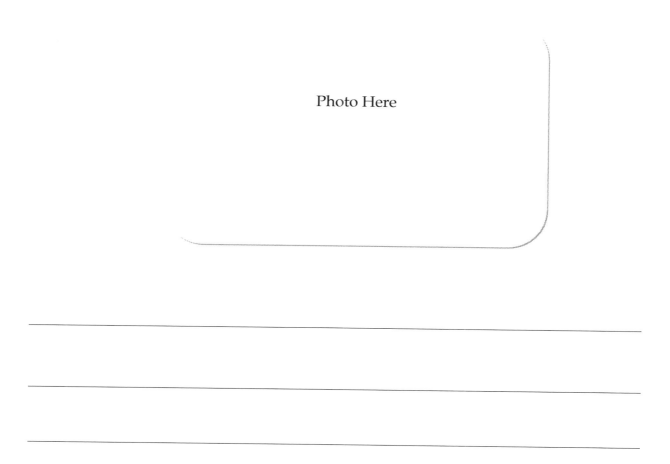

Photo Here

Our Puppy

Photo Here

Our Puppy

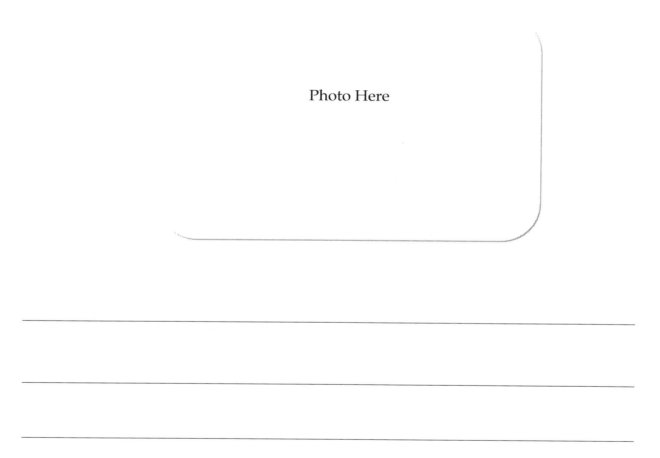

Photo Here

Our Puppy

Photo Here

Our Puppy

Photo Here

_____

_____

_____

Our Puppy

Photo Here

Our Puppy

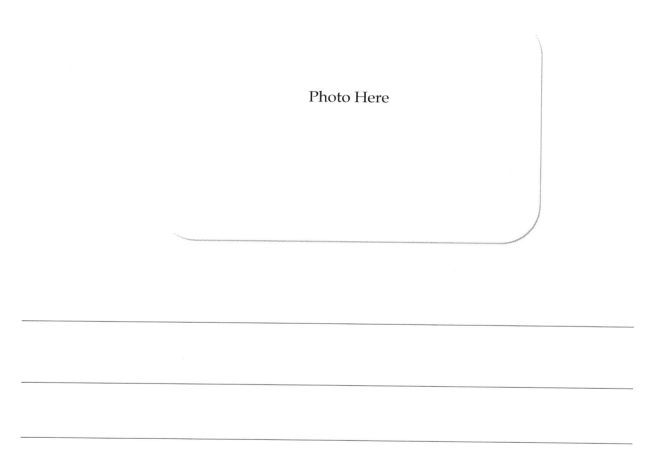

Photo Here

Our Puppy

Photo Here

Our Puppy

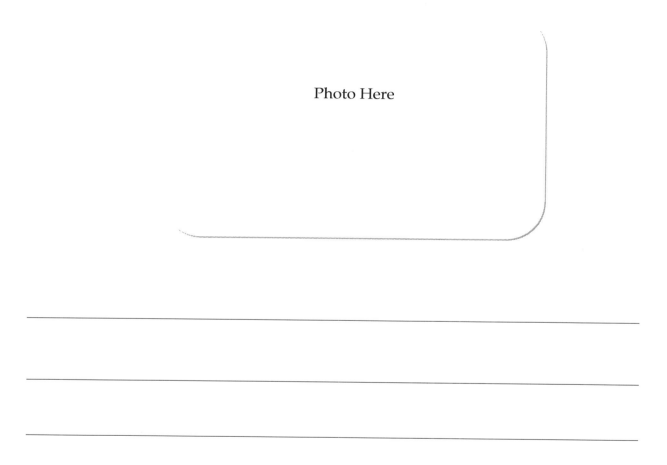

Photo Here

Our Puppy

Photo Here

Our Puppy

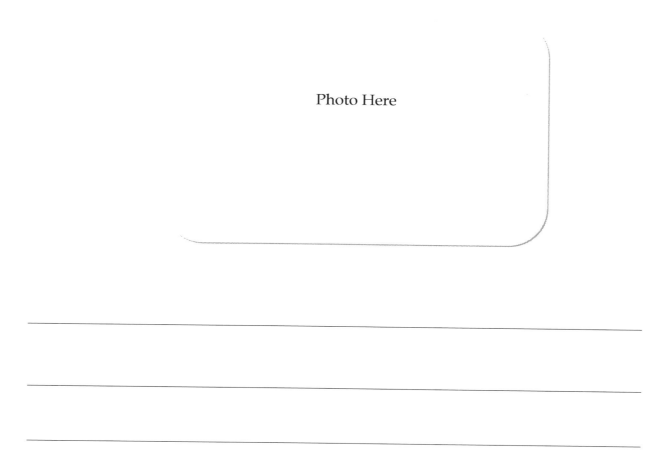

Photo Here

Our Puppy

Photo Here

_____

_____

_____

Our Puppy

Photo Here

Our Puppy

Photo Here

Our Puppy

Photo Here

Our Puppy

Photo Here

Our Puppy

Photo Here

Our Puppy

Photo Here

Our Puppy

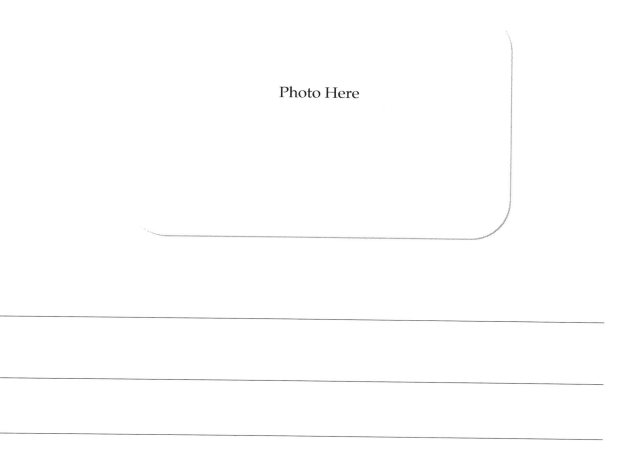

Photo Here

Our Puppy

Photo Here

Our Puppy

Photo Here

Our Puppy

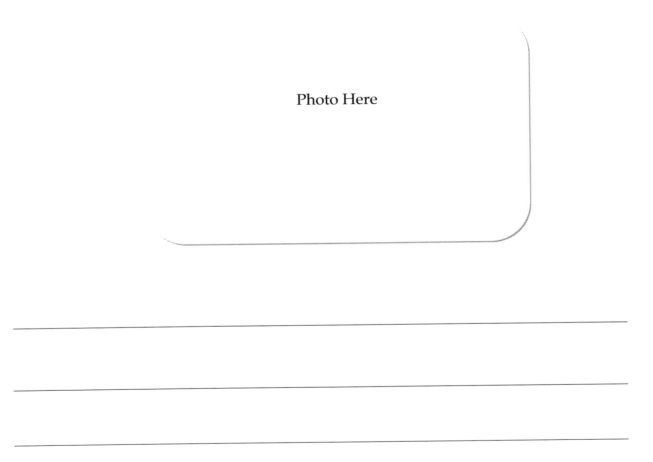

Photo Here

Our Puppy

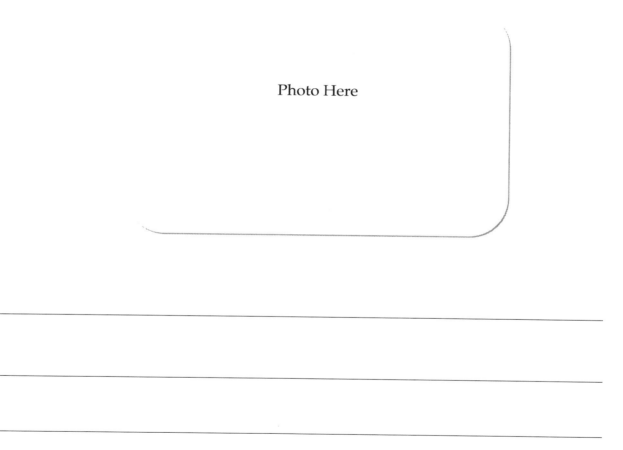

Photo Here

Our Puppy

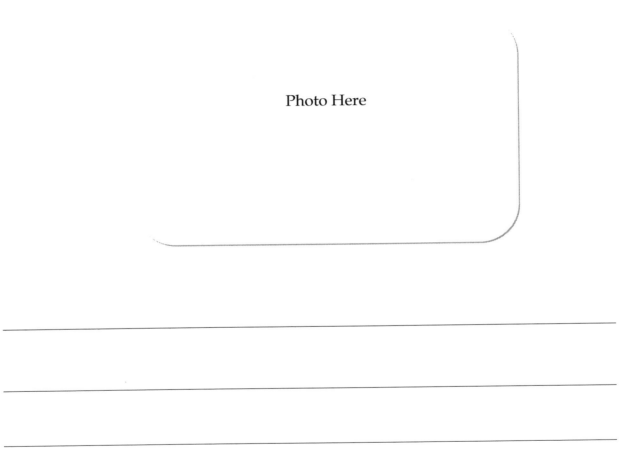

Photo Here

Our Puppy

Photo Here

_____

_____

_____

Our Puppy

Photo Here

_____

_____

_____

Our Puppy

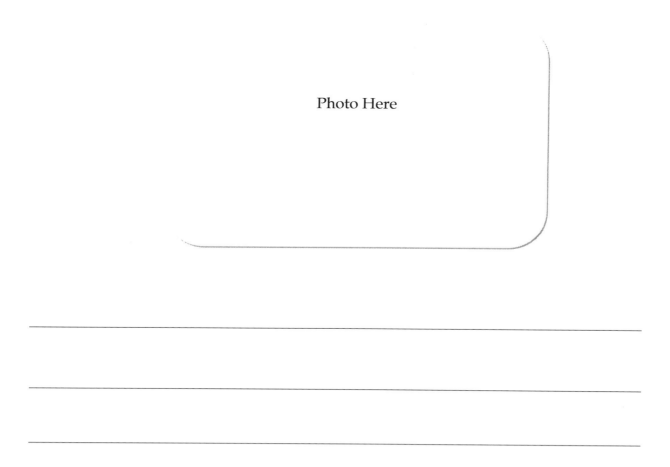

Photo Here

Our Puppy

Photo Here

_____

_____

_____

Our Puppy

Photo Here

All Grown Up

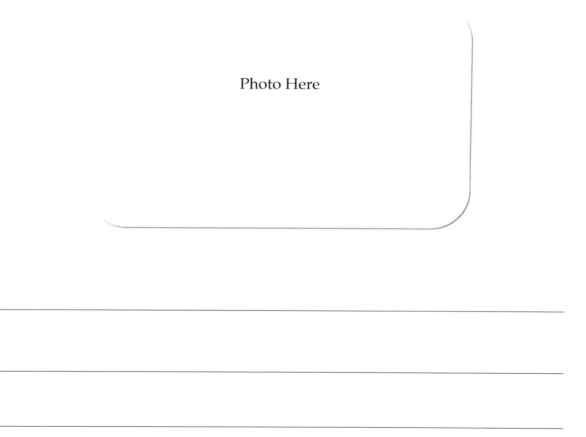

Photo Here

All Grown Up

Photo Here

All Grown Up

Photo Here

All Grown Up

Photo Here

All Grown Up

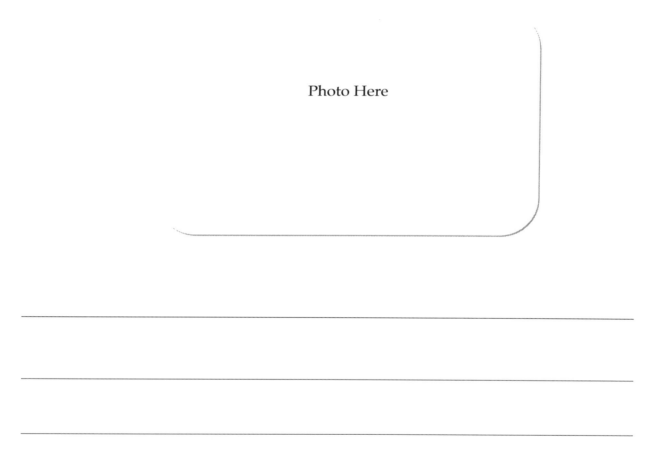

Photo Here

All Grown Up

Photo Here

All Grown Up

Photo Here

All Grown Up

Photo Here